Cork

Designed and produced by

JIM FEGAN

for

CORK CORPORATION

Text by

MARY LELAND

Project Committee:
Jim O'Donovan, Betty Dillon-Hall, Elizabeth Kidney, (Cork Corporation)
Pat Casey, Casey Communications
Mary Leland, Jim Fegan.

ISBN 0-902282-04-2

Photography by John Herriott,
Jim MacCarthy, Finbarr O'Connell, John Sheehan,
Examiner Publications, Michael Diggin, Bord Failte,
David Herriott, Inpho.

Origination by Pre-Press Reprographics,
Printed by Colourbooks Ltd.
1996

Cork

Corcaigh

Published by Cork Corporation Bardas Chorcaí

*M*o ghrá thú agus mo rún!
Tá do stácaí ar a mbonn,
tá do bha buí á gcrú;
is ar mo chroí atá do chumha
ná leigheasfadh Cúige Mumhan
ná Gaibhne Oileáin na bhFionn.
Go dtiocfaidh Art Ó Laoghaire chugham
ní scaipfidh ar mo cumha
atá i lár mo chroí á bhrú
dúnta suas go dlúth
mar a bheadh glas a bheadh ar thrúnc
's go raghadh an eochair amú.

My love and my dear!
Your stooks are standing,
your yellow cows milking;
On my heart is such sorrow
That all Munster could not cure it,
Nor the wisdom of the sages.
Till Art O'Leary returns
There will be no end to the grief
That presses down on my heart,
Closed up tight and firm
Like a trunk that is locked
And the key is mislaid.

(from: 'Caoineadh Airt Ui Laoghaire' by Eibhlín Dhubh Ní Chonaill, translated by Eilís Dillon as 'The Lament for Arthur O'Leary'. Art OLaoghaire is buried at Kilcrea Abbey, between Cork and Macroom.

ork's location at the mouth of a river and at the head of a harbour defines its character but not its history. The opportunities of its geography have been ready to the hands of its citizens through the ages. Future shock was made manifest here as long ago as 1177; since then the commercial and more recently the industrial - core of the city has flourished on a recognition of a particular sense of enterprise born out of topography.

It is not a question of an inward-looking sense of place, a self-awareness, a complacency (although these are indeed elements in the city's personality). Instead it is an out-reaching sense of placement, of alignment with other points of contact and of connection to the outside world.

Essential to this centralising vision of itself is the city's gateway identity. It opens outward from the countryside to the sea and countries - and markets - beyond; it opens inward from the sea to the countryside, the hinterland from which it has drawn both its earliest agricultural produce and its population.

Bringing in and sending out, therefore, have been the business of Cork almost since the city first climbed above the sedges of its watery roots. There is now some municipal and social merit in recognising that part of the charm of the place is the track of these earliest river channels, still visible here and there through the crust of the streets. Sanitised by affection, the lingering reeks in tiny curving laneways haunt the old photographs.

But charm is a doubtful enough asset to a city determined to grasp and to fashion its potential. A seductive ingredient in the make-up of a city, charm permits sentiment and endorses romanticism. It emphasises a native softness which, like the weather and the river and the marshy undergrowth which

surges into recalcitrant abundance at every opportunity of dereliction, neglect or regenerative sloth, provides a self-forgiving excuse.

In modern Cork it is preservation which is a crucial component of municipal policy and which has won a status readily maintained and expanded by the local authorities. Preservation values and protects the past, even while it moves with the times and with the European tenor of future management which seems uniquely suited to Cork's traditional municipal structure.

The achievement of the city of Cork and its people has been the mastering of its impulse for contentment - although there is much with which to be content - and the construction of its alliance with progress, with courage, and above all, with the future.

Despite its respect for the past, it is with the future that the city is now most deliberately engaged. The invitation of this assessment of Cork acknowledges the influence of what has gone before to make us what we are. What we will - or must - become is the challenge faced by the citizen and not for the first time.

The city of Cork, born out of fire and flood, has not had an easy history. It was once permissible to claim its origin in a monastic site of the seventh century; the foundation of St. Finbarr, however, had no enriching relic and did not harbour a shrine and there is a strong possibility that it didn't harbour St. Finbarr either. Such omissions cast doubt on the monastery (which did exist) as the foundation of the city. More compelling are the facts that a settlement of some kind existed before the monastery, that the area had a king, was mapped even if only as a marsh, and has a reference among the earliest of our legends.

It also had a trade, as did other pre-Christian Irish towns situated on harbours facing the Atlantic. It is no great irreverence to history's ethics to assume that the trade meant traffic and markets and import and export. Such a location would be an ideal site for a monastery with any aspiration to education, for it was to be from Europe that Ireland drew many of its greatest teachers and its scholastic reputation.

In Cork, for much of the first millennium, such visitors lived in peril. The settlement was subject to flooding (the monastery was built, wisely, on a hill); early records reveal that it was also subject to looting and burning. Regular well-planned raids by Vikings, Danes, and combinations of restless and ruthless Scandinavian tribes made life distinctly hazardous for the inhabitants through three centuries.

Such attacks - always, it seems, resulting in the burning of the town, monastery and church - occurred at intervals of only ten or twenty years. By the early 12th century however the raiders had surrendered the charms of plunder to the attractions of a settled life within a market town which also offered a safe, if often silted, anchorage.

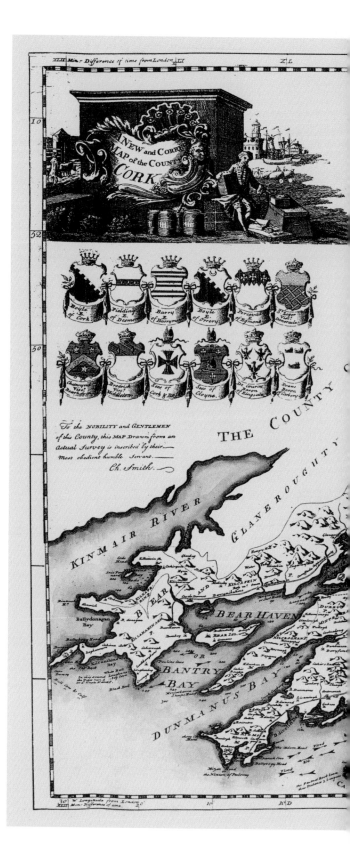

While the Danes and Norwegians blended into what has been called a race - the Ostmen - and settled down, the control of rival native kingships had teetered through the preceding hundred years. Their contests often reflected competing ecclesiastical interests. The church and monastery of St. Finbarr became significant in the fellowship of Munster churches and the foundation's status is indicated by its presence in the literature of the time.

When the King of Munster died in Cork in 1118 religious deliberations led to the division of the county of Cork into the three dioceses of Cork, Cloyne and Ross, definitions which have persisted, with attendant controversy from era to era, to this day.

Ireland itself was divided. The provinces and their different kings demanded allegiances which decided territorial control. One of Cork county's most famous buildings, the castle at Blarney, is spoken of still as a stronghold of the MacCarthy line which ruled what was then the Kingdom of South Munster. The Dal Cais interests had lost their disputed hold on the city by 1118, and for some years after that Cork struggled through the rivalries of the O'Briens of Thomond, the O'Connors of Connaught and the MacCarthys of Desmond. The Desmond faction enjoyed a short-lived triumph, for in 1171 Dermot MacCarthy surrendered "his" city of Cork to Henry ll, the invading Norman King of England who installed a governor and garrison in what was by then a walled town.

This submission by MacCarthy may have been a holding tactic and did not win unanimous native approval. In 1173 Cork's Irish-Ostmen faction sent a fleet of thirty-two ships to challenge the Normans of Youghal; the Cork Ships were defeated, but MacCarthy also faced the scorn of his own son Cormac and his efforts to regain both territory and kingship only ended with his death, in 1185, as he besieged the city for the second time.

This tumultuous twelfth century is the era on which Cork now relies for much of its history and character. It is the demarcation point for the modern era, the time of the city's charter (although the first charter referred to the Kingdom of Cork, meaning the greater Cork area, a version of the modern county) when Henry ll distinguished between the city itself and the Cantred of the Ostmen. The town was already fortified, the Ostmen had enhanced the trading community, and the royal decrees guaranteed or seemed to guarantee, two crucial factors which were to distinguish and to characterise the city of Cork for the future.

These were first the acceptance of certain commercial privileges which endorsed the city's license to trade, its right to establish crafts guilds and to raise tolls, and second, even more significantly, the right to municipal self-government. Given that this right still depended on ultimate acknowledgement of royal authority and the payment of a stipulated rent to the crown, its lasting importance (although of course this altered in degree and in kind through the centuries) was the exemption from what have been called "the servile burdens" of the feudal system.

Cork had retained, to an extent almost unique in those times, the power to shape its own environment.

This municipal structure was to be maintained, although sometimes threatened and frequently vulnerable, through the centuries. Allied to the city's role as a port and the development of its import and export trade, it was to remain the underlying characteristic of survival.

Survival was a particular skill in those times. The Black Death and frequent visitations of pestilence, famine with its attendant diseases, the recurrence of flooding with the destruction of bridges as well as buildings, the ruination consequent on fire - these were the lot of Cork through the ages as they were of other towns in other countries.

They were matched in horror and despair by political variations: wars both great and local, internal, tribal and international purged and plundered the growing city. Pirates, embargoes, sieges and riots all afflicted Cork. Religious differences took on their bloody political role: abbeys, friaries, schools and hospitals changed hands and disappeared.

The walls, despite the attempts of the governors to maintain them without putting Queen Elizabeth to any greater cost than the use of her shovels and spades, crumbled and began their final collapse after the Siege of Cork in 1690. Descriptions of that event indicate a city large by the conventions of that time; seventy years earlier the great burning of Cork was said to have resulted in "the utter ruin and consumption of a rich and wealthy Cittie".

Within the walls a settled prosperous life went on. Outside roved the bands of the disaffected, effectively besieging the burghers and claiming varying allegiances as the tides of war, plantation and retribution flowed around and through the still-growing town. The mighty gladiators of the European arena touched these shores, marched through these alleyways, dined in vanished, once-gilded mansions in streets still familiar to the local ken.

They were rivalled by the local heroes, the warlords of Muskerry, Carbery, Kerricurrihy and Kinelea, of Imokilly and Orrery and Duhallow and Oliehain, the mighty and often ruthless leaders of Gaelic society. If the tidal river was one force governing the fortunes of the city, the tides of war had their impact too; rebellion divided the city against itself, and while the names of the burghers and bailiffs and trading families of the medieval city can still be found among its modern citizens, here also echo the names of the native lordships and those made native by marriage, time and conquest.

The MacCarthys and the Desmonds resound though the centuries, and the war-torn hinterland of Muskerry was uncomfortably close to the city; indeed, the towns of Blarney, Ballincollig and Carrigaline and the village of Carrigrohane are almost part of greater modern Cork. The friary at Kilcrea is an easy journey to the west and a landmark which the MacCarthys in their movement eastwards left behind them as the Muskerry claimants gradually encircled the frightened city.

To the south the Courcys at Kinsale and the Barrys of Rincorran and Inishannon sought supremacy and autonomy in their lands; to the east the Roches and the Cauntons (or Condons) fought over Glanworth, Kilworth, Ballyhooley and Fermoy. They fought with a savagery and a persistence maintained through generation after generation. They were fighting not against a common, colonising foe, but against their fellow-countrymen. Yet in the end it was the coloniser who defeated their claims and ended, almost entirely, their hold on the kingdom of Cork.

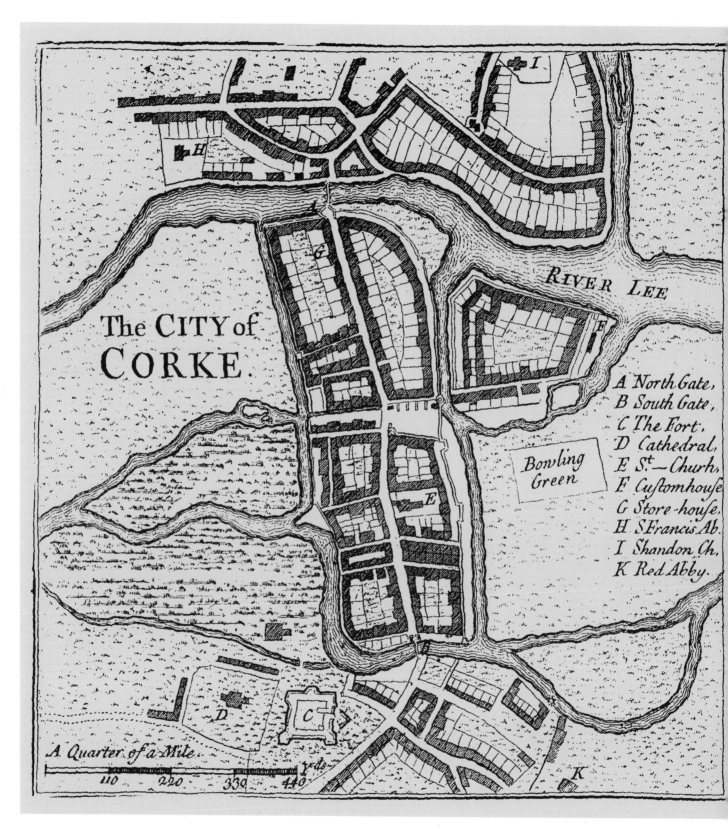

The CITY of CORKE.

RIVER LEE

Bowling
Green

A North Gate,
B South Gate,
C The Fort,
D Cathedral,
E St — Churh,
F Customhouse
G Store-house,
H S.Francis Ab.
I Shandon Ch.
K Red Abby.

A Quarter of a Mile.
110   220   330   440

The reign of Henry VIII saw the Dublin-based administration growing uneasy about the decentralised power structures still enjoyed, and perhaps from their point of view abused, in Cork. The accession of Elizabeth I, and later the plantation of the province of Munster of which the Kingdom of Cork made up a great part, put an end to the ambitions of the Gaelic lords, finally denying the heroism of the last of the Desmonds and the unappeasable interests of the remnants of Gaelic society.

The settlers evolved a new power structure; from their ranks emerged men such as Richard Boyle, the first Earl of Cork. From this time on the city and the county experienced to the fullest degree the meaning of both temporal and spiritual colonisation. The Reformation led to a defining religious split between the English administration and the Irish people, and this is also the period from which the last vestiges of the ancient lineages of Gaelic civilisation can be seen, totally committed to the pursuit of ancient feuds.

What had been lost? John A. Murphy, Emeritus Professor of Irish History at University College, Cork, has written, in his introduction to *"Cork: History and Society"* (Geography Publications, Dublin, 1993) of the exiled MacCarthy lady called to the window in France to watch a victory procession led by Louis the XIV, the Sun King: "I have seen MacCarthy entering Blarney," was her disdainful reply, "and what can Paris offer to equal that?"

History will always have its arguments. Scholarship exists on dispute, research, interpretation. Heroes and heroines of one era vanish in the dust of another. Yet they leave their mark even in their absences; exile has a cumulative power and offers its own legends like the seal of a vanished lease, an imprint on an inherited memory.

There is no contention about the two-fold nature of the survival of this merchant city: the constant feature has been the maintenance of a kind of administrative independence allied to the management of and exploitation of the port. The river re-appears at every juncture of Cork's development. Its flux undercut the walls and repairs required quays and piers and inevitably bridges. These in time altered the location of the anchorages; a benign harbour for ships was once contained within what is now a street, called Castle Street because indeed the waterway was guarded by a castle at each end, whose defensive purposes gradually gave way to the commerce of port dues and tolls.

The English poet Spenser, writing while waiting here for an advancement which never came, gave Cork a description of itself which has remained in the water-logged lexicon of local history:

"The spreading Lee, that like an island fayre
Encloseth Corke with his divided flood".

It is tempting to think that the divided flood was the river as we know it to-day, its two channels enclosing the city centre. In fact it was a much-divided flood, with streams and gullies winding in haphazard but determining courses.

The Anglo-Norman city had at least sixteen towers on its walls; there was within it a King's Castle (demolished in the 17th century to make way for a court-house) and a Queen's Castle, but it was surrounded as well as bisected by water. As Cork spread beyond the walls and as the walls themselves disintegrated the stone was used both as ballast for ships lying further down-river and as building materials for better quays. Those who owned or drained marshland were charged with bridging the different islands.

utside the walls there were buildings such as monasteries, hospitals (a leper hospital on both northern and southern slopes), friaries of which only one, the Augustinian Red Abbey, has left a trace, although the convent at St. Marie's of the Isle is on the site of a 13th century Dominican friary, where Edmund Mortimer, Earl of March and enemy of John of Gaunt, died at Christmas, 1381.

Domestic building was concentrated for centuries on sites already built on. Cork lacks great street-scapes today and there are few indications of private or municipal planning of the kind which has given Dublin its Georgian vistas; the river is the explanation. To build meant to drain; to build with any sense of civic perspective involved costs greater than those normally associated with the acquisition of land and the price of materials and labour.

The river was an opportunity, or at least an influence, too. If Cork has a continental air today, as many insist it has, it reflects the city's open-ness to the Mediterranean, to Europe, from those times in which an export of wool and hides was matched by the import, from the great cities of France and Spain, of wines and spices and silks; from the days in which departing monks yielded in return the foreign scholarship of the vast mainland.

That reminiscent side-long view of a gable or an oriel window or simply a phrase or an inflected idiom is stirred by a gust from a history of sanctuary, bloodstained and even anarchic in itself, which the chateaux of France and the abbeys of Spain or Belgium or the armies of other greater causes offered to the dispossessed of Ireland, and of Munster.

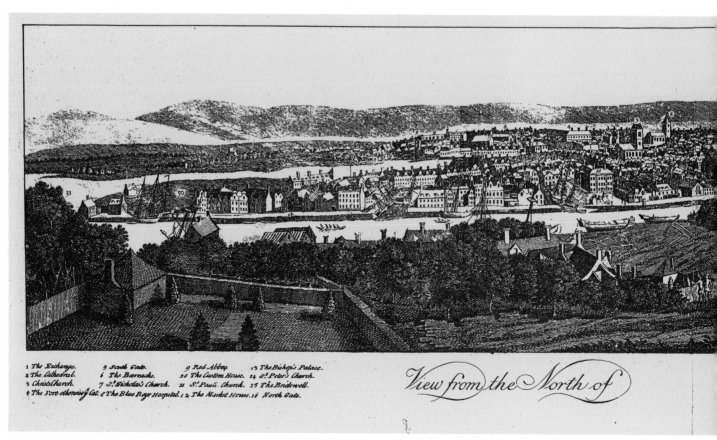

1 The Exchange.   5 South Gate.   9 Red Abbey   13 The Bishop's Palace.
2 The Cathedral.   6 The Barracks.   10 The Custom House. 14 S.t Peter's Church.
3 Christ Church.   7 S.t Nicholas's Church. 11 S.t Paul's Church. 15 The Bridewell.
4 The Fort othawise Cat. 8 The Blue Boys Hospital. 12 The Market House. 16 North Gate.

View from the North of

The victor Saxon, the baffled French, met the Irish as soldiers or pilgrims, as claimants, allies, or provocateurs, and above all as refugees. It was from Cork, from the old jetties at the Lower Road near the present Kent Station, that Sarsfield led the last few thousand of his followers to France; it was from Cork, from a later version of the same quays, that those who would flee the Great Famine took ship for Liverpool, or else went to the nearby railway station at Summer Hill to take the train to Cobh and their passage to America and Canada.

And it was from the city and port of Cork that the agricultural industry of Munster made its way to the markets of the world. For the royal navy there was victualling, with beef and mutton and pork the prime demand. The fortunes of Cork's merchant princes were built on the shambles, the slaughter-houses and tanneries of Blackpool, and the offal left behind when the navy took the best of every carcass. To this day the citizens relish kidneys and liver, tripe and the blood sausage known as drisheen, pork skirts and trotters. The best restaurants are not too grand to serve these items, to dress sweetbreads or to extol the pleasure of corned and spiced beef, or to pretend that the use of lamb in an Irish Stew is an improvement on the original ingredient of scrag-end of mutton.

Evolution of this kind was not incidental or capricious but reflected a commercial consciousness which, when allied to the resources of the huge agricultural hinterland, produced much of the city we recognise today by the early 19th century. The walls were gone. The streams were increasingly being turned into streets. Theatres rather than gibbets provided the public entertainment.

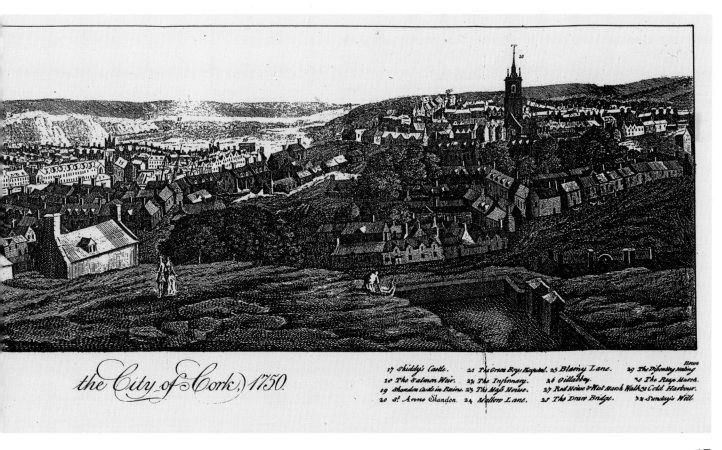

the City of Cork, 1750.

17 Skiddy's Castle. 21 The Green Boys Hospital. 25 Blarney Lane. 29 The Dishouse Booking House
18 The Salmon Weir. 22 The Infirmary. 26 Gillabbey. 30 The Rope Marsh.
19 Shandon Castle in Ruins. 23 The Mass House. 27 Red House & Nut March Walk 31 Cold Harbour.
20 St Anne Shandon. 24 Mallow Lane. 28 The Draw Bridge. 32 Sunday's Well.

*N*ew building took on a gracious, settled style, and suburbs began to link the population and business of the city with the villas of the grander merchants on the surrounding hills.

Through the years also the army barracks in the city, the Admiralty in Cobh and the varying fortunes of the developing industries coloured the hectic politics of an era which bridges the gap between the late medieval town and the modern city. There were other channels to be bridged. One was the continuing division in the city between the religion practiced by most of the administration, landlords and nobility and that adhered to by the mass of the population: as K.W. Nicholls writes in his chapter on *"The Development of Lordship in County Cork"* (Cork: History and Society, Dublin, 1993) the Irish were offered, and accepted, the Counter - Reformation before being offered the Reformation in any meaningful way.

The other gap was one of racial consciousness, the divide between the diminishing Gaelic, Irish-speaking and by now mostly rural people, and the flourishing English -language culture of the town. Both these divisions had, separately and together, a crucial political significance for Cork, although they were not unique to the city. Defining factors in the changes at the beginning of this century, both have left an imaginative legacy in song, story and street-name as well as being the continuing focus of scholarship and analysis.

Examination of the citizenry is no new science in Cork, however. "The genus man is gregarious by instinct; the species Corkonian by temperament" wrote B.A.Cody in 1859 in *"The River Lee, Cork and the Corkonians"* (London, 1859), describing the people of Cork as mercurial but fun-loving, to whom the excitement of society is absolutely essential. More interesting to the visitor perhaps is Cody's assurance that "another trait in their multiform and many-hued character is the marked partiality they seem to evince for strangers. Speak with an English, Scotch, or foreign accent, wear a sleek moustache - in a word be a stranger of presentable appearance, and you will immediately have the *entree* to the best society in Cork."

This welcoming characteristic is sadly offset by Cody's assertion that nowhere did class exclusivity exist with greater intensity than in the society of Cork "where the *esprit de caste* is maintained with a Brahminical vigour".

Cody was accurate, however, in his jovial metaphor of the society of Cork as one in which everyone must have his social rank scratched upon him, as if the city were "one vast weigh- house".

The figure is borrowed from the trade which had come to dominate Cork during the late 18th and early 19th centuries and which is still recognised as the source of its prosperity in those years.

While, from the seventeenth century onwards, places like Blackpool were centres of economic success in the shape of slaughterhouses, glue-factories, tanneries, chandlers, salters, coopers, soap-makers and butchers, all built on the cattle trade, it was the weigh-house at Shandon which focussed the mercantile attention of the city. Here was the centre of the butter trade, here was established the Cork Butter Market (its portico decorated with a cows' head still stands outside what has become the Shandon Crafts Centre) and here held sway the Committee of Merchants which regulated the trade and imposed a stringent and ultimately world-famous system of quality control and marking.

At the same time Cork's local industry included the production of textiles, ship-building, brewing and distilling. The fortunes to be made encouraged an ambitious Catholic middle- class, joining if not replacing what were once described as "the opulent gentlemen" of Cork, and with them many of the fine houses still visible on the suburban fringes of the city, and the streetscapes of imposing hillside terraces.

Although often self-important and ambitious, these men adhered to ideals of the cultured life which influenced their civic attitudes and which have left their mark on the city we know today. The Grand Tour was undertaken, and the luxurious suburbs of Tivoli and Montenotte, the gardens of Lakelands and Vernon Mount, were the result. Philanthropy was recognised as a duty rather than a hobby: the Art Gallery, the City Library, the endowment of schools and hospitals and parks all enriched the personality of the city in which such people made their fortunes.

New bridges and the arrival of the railway lines allowed further expansion. Important public buildings were erected, from the University College buildings on the Western Road (Queen Victoria herself watched the installation of her commemorative image to the gable of the new college in 1849) to the Cork Savings Bank at the top of the South Mall. Churches, hotels, the new Customs House, hospitals and schools were all designed with a strong sense of civic grandeur; slobland was reclaimed and new quays built, while at the same time slum clearances and the building of artisan dwellings foreshadowed the major urban changes of the twentieth century.

For close on three miles above Cork the river runs slow and smooth as if reluctant to meet the sea. Pleasant meadows border the stream, meadows in a wide valley, the gateway to the west... You can walk the whole length of its course without seeing even a village for, from Cork to its source, there is not a hamlet on its banks.

A house here and there, a cottage by a bridge. Such lovely bridges, too. As you follow the banks there is just sufficient track to give you confidence. It may be cattle or sheep, or even rabbits, perhaps the footsteps of a labourer going to and from his work that has tempered the growing of the grass. The glory of the river is yours.

(from "Lovely is the Lee" by Robert Gibbings, London, 1944)

y Royal Charter the Kingdom of Cork was granted to Robert Fitzstephen and Milo de Cogan, but the City of Cork and the Cantred of the Ostmen were retained by Henry..... The Kingdom of Cork given to his followers Fitzstephen and de Cogan was a present of a very doubtful value. It may be compared to a present of a hive of bees, which in the process of being made really useful, might occasionally involve the recipients in nasty complications, which in fact it did.

(from "The Economic History of Cork from the Earliest Times to the Act of Union" by Wm. O'Sullivan, Cork University Press, 1937)

*I have sought to discover
a haven of rest,
Where the sun sinks by night
in the land of the West;
I have dwelt with the red man
in green forest bowers,
Or the wild-rolling prairie,
bespangled with flowers.
I have hied to the north,
where the hardy pine grows,
'Mid the wolf and the bear,
and the bleak winter snows;
I have roamed through all
climates, but none could I see
Like the green hills of Cork
and my home by the Lee.
Beautiful city, beautiful city,
Beautiful city, the pride of the Lee*

(from "The Green Hills of Cork",
John FitzGerald, Bard of The Lee,
1913)

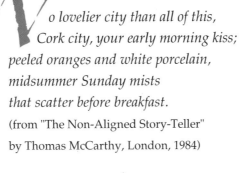

o lovelier city than all of this,
Cork city, your early morning kiss;
peeled oranges and white porcelain,
midsummer Sunday mists
that scatter before breakfast.
(from "The Non-Aligned Story-Teller"
by Thomas McCarthy, London, 1984)

27

*T*he road led past the military barrack on the brow of the hill
and then down a dirt track called Fever Hospital Hill to the
brewery, before climbing again through slums to the top of
other hill. But the view from Fever Hospital Hill was astonish-
, and often delayed me when I was already late. The cathedral
er and Shandon steeple, all limestone and blue sandstone, soared
the edge of the opposite hill, and the hillside, terraced to the top
h slums, stood so deep that I could see every lane in it, and when
light moved across it on a Spring day, the whole hillside seemed
sway like a field of corn, and sometimes when there was no wind
stir the clouds I could hear it murmuring to itself like a hive of
s.

m "An Only Child", Frank O'Connor, 1961)

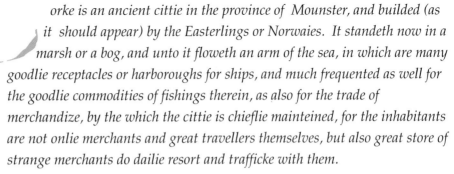

orke is an ancient cittie in the province of Mounster, and builded (as it should appear) by the Easterlings or Norwaies. It standeth now in a marsh or a bog, and unto it floweth an arm of the sea, in which are many goodlie receptacles or harboroughs for ships, and much frequented as well for the goodlie commodities of fishings therein, as also for the trade of merchandize, by the which the cittie is chieflie mainteined, for the inhabitants are not onlie merchants and great travellers themselves, but also great store of strange merchants do dailie resort and trafficke with them.

(from "The Annals of Cork", Caulfield's Council Book of the Corporation of Cork 1870)

33

After service they generally betake themselves to a public walk, called the Mall, which is no more than a very ill-paved quay upon one of their canals with a row of trees on one side, and houses on the other. It is a pleasure, however, to see that they are filling up this canal, and several others, where the water, having no current, must have become noxious to the air in hot weather.

(from "A Philosophical Survey of the South of Ireland" by Thomas Campbell, 1778)

*F*inally it may be asked, was Cork, that is modern Cork, founded at all in the ordinary meaning of the word. as used when considering the foundation of a monastery, where direct succession and traditions may be maintained for centuries ?..... St Finbarr founded a monastery. The Norse, influenced by certain motives, founded a settlement in a marsh around the river, probably in the site mentioned already. The existence of Cork today, a city of substantial dimensions and commercial importance is due to circumstances to which the two latter incidents contributed little or nothing, even though its location has been very materially influenced by the site of the Ostman Settlement.

(from "The Economic History of Cork", O'Sullivan 1937)

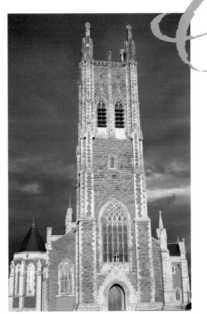

*nce the three of us met
on Patrick's Bridge after
Corkery and O'Faolain
had attended a service at the
cathedral, and when O'Faolain
went off in his home-spun suit,
swinging his ash-plant, Corkery
looked after him as I had once seen
him look after Terence MacSwiney
and said: "There goes a born
literary man!". For months I was
mad with jealousy.*
(from "An Only Child", Frank
O'Connor 1961)

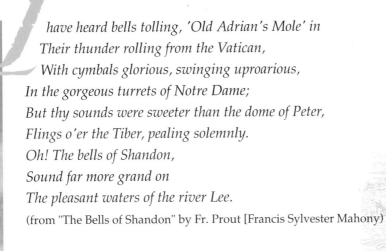

I have heard bells tolling, 'Old Adrian's Mole' in
Their thunder rolling from the Vatican,
   With cymbals glorious, swinging uproarious,
In the gorgeous turrets of Notre Dame;
But thy sounds were sweeter than the dome of Peter,
Flings o'er the Tiber, pealing solemnly.
Oh! The bells of Shandon,
Sound far more grand on
The pleasant waters of the river Lee.

(from "The Bells of Shandon" by Fr. Prout [Francis Sylvester Mahony)

1601

Sir George Carew to the Privy Council: To strengthen this town of Cork I have been of late casting up certain earth works, but that your Lordship may know that I have a care of her Majies person, the charge thereof is defrayed 'tho unwillingly yielded unto, by the town and county, each of these according me 200 labourers, the Queen being at no other charge than the use of her shovels and spades.

(from Caulfield's Council Book, State Papers)

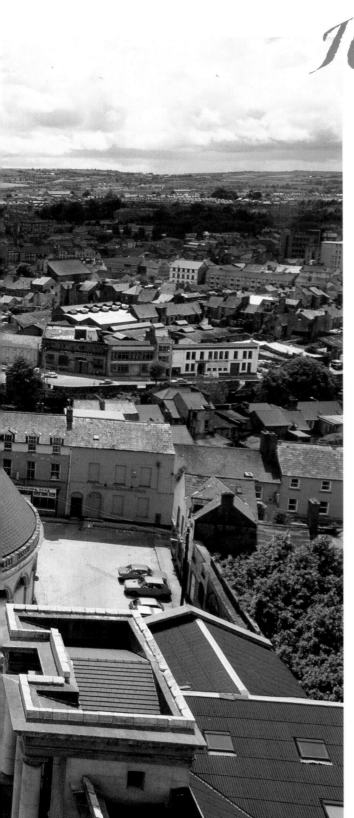

*T*he leaves of the trees along the Mardyke were
astir and whispering in the sunlight. A team of
cricketers passed, agile young men in flannels
and blazers, one of them carrying the long green wicket-bag.
In a quiet bystreet a German band of five players in faded
uniforms and with battered brass instruments was playing to
an audience of street arabs and leisurely messenger boys. A
maid in a white cap and apron was watering a box of plants on
a sill which shone like a slab of limestone in the warm glare.
From another window open to the air came the sound of a
piano, scale after scale rising to the treble.

(from "A Portrait of the Artist as a Young Man" by James Joyce, 1916)

o walk in the city is as good as a tour through Europe. You look down one side street and you see Dieppe, another alongside of it and you are reminded of Oxford, another and you think of Italy. And the city also possesses a splendour of its own. Where else, may I ask, of an evening but by Patrick's Bridge will you see lavender-coloured mullet weaving their courses among the reflected scarlet neon signs of Denny's Bacon and Paddy Whiskey?

(from "Sweet Cork of Thee" by Robert Gibbings, 1952)

hey may talk about London, and Paris and Milan,
And Constinantinople, the pride o' the Turk
But away in the south of our own little Island
Is a place that excels them - its name it is Cork;
With its whiskey, drisheens, and fine girls in plenty,
Jackeens and fat pork in the sweet River Lee,
And the "dyke" where all lovers from fifteen to twenty,
Whisper "Cork is the Eden for you love and me"

(from the Poetical Works of John Fitzgerald, 1913)

To this day the citizens relish kidney and liver, tripe and the blood sausage known as drisheen, pork skirts and trotters; like Arbutus Lodge, the best restaurants are not too grand to serve these items, to avoid sweetbreads or to extol the pleasure of corned and spiced beef, or to pretend that the use of lamb in an Irish Stew is an improvement to the original ingredient of scrag-end of mutton.

*I*n the drained glass,
In the barman's smile as you
Slowly grow absent

As in mirrors that repeat
A childhood nightmare,
No reflection.

You say, we live in Babel.
You say, we live in Hell.
Nobody disagrees.

You stare in the mirror
And childhood is very near,
A thirsted-for oblivion.

Humphrey! Allow me to
Buy this man a drink.

("Long Valley Vignette", from "The
Ordinary House of Love" by Theo
Dorgan, Galway, 1990)

To-day
*   Is the feast day of Saint Anne*
Pray for me
I am the madwoman of Cork

Yesterday
In Castle Street
I saw two goblins at my feet
I saw a horse without a head
Carrying the dead
To the graveyard
Near Turner's Cross.

I am the madwoman of Cork
No one talks to me
....

And if I die now don't touch me.
I want to sail in a long boat
From here to Roche's Point
And there I will anoint the sea
With oil of alabaster.

I am the madwoman of Cork
And to-day is the feast day of
Saint Anne.
Feed me.

(from "The Madwoman of Cork",
from "The Woodburners"
by Patrick Galvin, 1973)

In town, women wore hats and gloves or fringed black shawls. There were horses and drays carrying coal through the cobbled streets where ran narrow rail tracks which would later catapult us from our bicycles. There were familiar characters like Andy Gaw, who might give you sixpence with his handshake, and a sweet shop called Hadji Bey's. My mother went into town to auctions and to meet her friends in Thompsons in Patrick Street, with its tiered silver cakestand, or in the Green Door Restaurant over Barters Travel Agents where we sat at damask-covered tables. The tables were small to accommodate intimate conversation.

(from "A Cork Girlhood" by Isabel Healy, The Cork Anthology, Cork, 1993)

The reasonable conclusion seems to be that no settlement or city of any consequence existed on or near the site of Cork before the arrival of St. Finbarr.... on or about the beginning of the 7th century.......Tradition places the site of St. Finbarr's church where the present day Protestant Cathedral is situated, and the monastic settlement as extending from this along the district north of the Lough, extending on both sides of what is now known as Gilabbey Street and College Road, about as far as the locality now occupied by University College Cork.

(from The Economic History of Cork, William O'Sullivan, 1937)

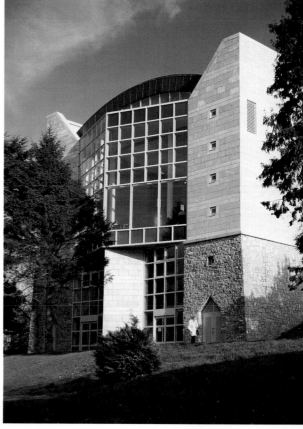

*I*t is no great surprise, for example, that the food sciences are significant study areas at University College, Cork, where both the Faculty of Food Science and Technology and the National Food Biotechnology Centre operate international centres for education, research and training for industry which harnesses traditional resources with the most contemporary developments in both production and marketing.

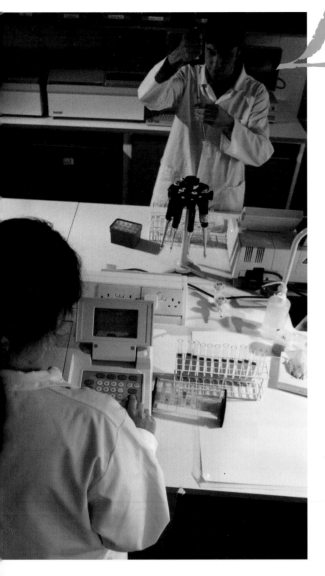

I pick a magnifying glass from your desk
& hold it to a haze of men
bowed over the jigsaw puzzles of galley trays.

You confer with Dan Hannigan.
I wonder at the results of a half century
of nicotine on his right index finger.

Through zig-zag bars of an old-fashioned elevator
I have just spotted the ascending head
& Humpty Dumpty body of Donnie Conroy.

He will be broken by drink
& his daughter's death.
Her face is now smiling from his desk.

You turn and escort me to the letterpress.
Mr. Lane punches my name into a shiny lead
& declares hereafter it is eternal.

The names of Dan Hannigan, Owen Lane, Donnie Conroy -
I could go on forever invoking the dead -
were set deep in a boy

impressed by the common raised type on the 3rd floor
of Eagle Printing Company, 15 Oliver Plunkett Street,
in the summer-still, ticking heart of Cork City.

("Setting the Type" from "Southward" by Greg Delanty, Dublin, 1992)

The Library is one of the newest buildings
at the Cork Regional Technical College,
where the many departments include a
School of Printing.

The National Microelectronics Research Centre - located, in another example of inspired preservation, in the old river-side maltings buildings of an otherwise vanished brewery.

*H*e lived in a small suburban house on Gardiner's Hill with his mother and sister, surrounded by books and pictures. Over the mantelpiece was a large water colour of his own of a man with a scythe on Fair Hill overlooking the great panorama of the river valley. Inside the door of the living room was a bust of him by his friend, Joe Higgins which - if my memory of it is correct - is the only likeness of him that captures all his charm. He presided over his little group from a huge Morris chair with a detachable desk that he had made for himself (he was a craftsman, having been brought up to the trade, and once told me in his oracular way that "nobody had ever met a stupid carpenter" which I later found to be untrue).

(from "An Only Child", Frank O'Connor, 1961)

Tá Tír na nÓg ar chúl an tí,
    Tír álainn trína chéile,
    Lucht ceithre cos ag siúl na slí
Gan bróga orthu ná léine,
Gan Béarla acu ná Gaeilge.

Ach fásann clóca ar gach droim
Sa tír seo trína chéile,
Is labhartar teanga ar chúl an tí
Nár thuig aon fhear ach Aesop,
Is tá sé siúd sa chré anois.

Tá cearca ann is ál sicín,
Is lacha righin mhothaolach,
Is gadhar mór dubh mar namhaid sa tír
Ag drannadh le gach éinne,
Is cat ag crú na gréine.

Sa chúinne thiar tá banc dramhaíl'
Is iontaisí an tsaoil ann,
Coinnleoir, búclaí, seanhata tuí,
Is trúmpa balbh néata,
Is citeal bán mar ghé ann.

Is ann a thagann tincéirí
Go naofa trína chéile,
Tá gaol acu le cúl an tí,
Is bíd ag iarraidh déirce
Ar chúl gach tí in Éirinn.

Ba mhaith liom bheith ar cúl an tí
Sa doircheacht go déanach
Go bhfeicinn ann ar chuairt gealaí
An t-ollaimhín sin Aesop
Is é ina phúca léannta.

("Cúl an Tí" from "Eireaball Spideoige" by
Seán Ó Riordáin , Baile Átha Cliath, 1952)

he genus man is gregarious by instinct; the species Corkonian by temperament. Another trait in their multiform and many hued character is the marked partiality they seem to evince for strangers. Speak with an English, Scotch or foreign accent, wear a sleek moustache - in a word be a stranger of presentable appearance and you will immediately have the entree to the best society in Cork.

(from "The River Lee, Cork and the Corkonians" by B.A. Cody, London, 1859)

We lived in the stories of children's classics and contemporary Irish and American writers. Maura Laverty was spoken of with affection and we read "The Cottage In The Bog" and the "Little Red Hen" "and books by Eilís Dillon, but the greatest favourites were Patrick Lynch, Laura Ingalls Wilder, Eloise and the "Caty stories"

("A Cork Girlhood" by Isabel Healy from The Cork Anthology, 1993)

The 27 acres of pleasure grounds surrounding Fota House, the splendid Regency mansion designed by Richard Morrison, form the centrepiece of the estate on [Fo]ta Island. Sheltered by the inlet of Lough Mahon and pro[tec]ted by belts of trees the island provides very favourable [con]ditions for sheltered species.

The Smith Barry family began planting the garden in the 1820s, some of the oldest trees date from this period and the layout has changed little in 200 years.

Collections of plants from Chile, Japan and China are particularly well represented and specimens have been planted individually so that they can be admired from every angle.

(from 'The Hidden Gardens of Ireland' by Marianne Heron. 1995)

*I*n the year 1811 Daniel Maclise was
born in Cork. While still a young man he
painted four of the frescoes in the house of
Lords. Since then the British Constitution has
been maintained in an aura of Cork colours.

(from "Lovely is the Lee" by Robert Gibbings, 1944)

It seemed entirely natural to me when one day the doors were flung open (in the middle of a matinee of "A Royal Divorce") to allow the acrid smoke of the Battle of Waterloo to creep out and into Half Moon Street, and pouring out through its pungent clouds came the entire Napoleonic Army, sometimes called the Butter Exchange Band... hastening across to the Alaska Bar for foaming pints quaffed with rolling eyes and hearty moustache-sucking in the middle of the street.

(from "Vive Moi!" by Sean O Faolain, London, 1965)

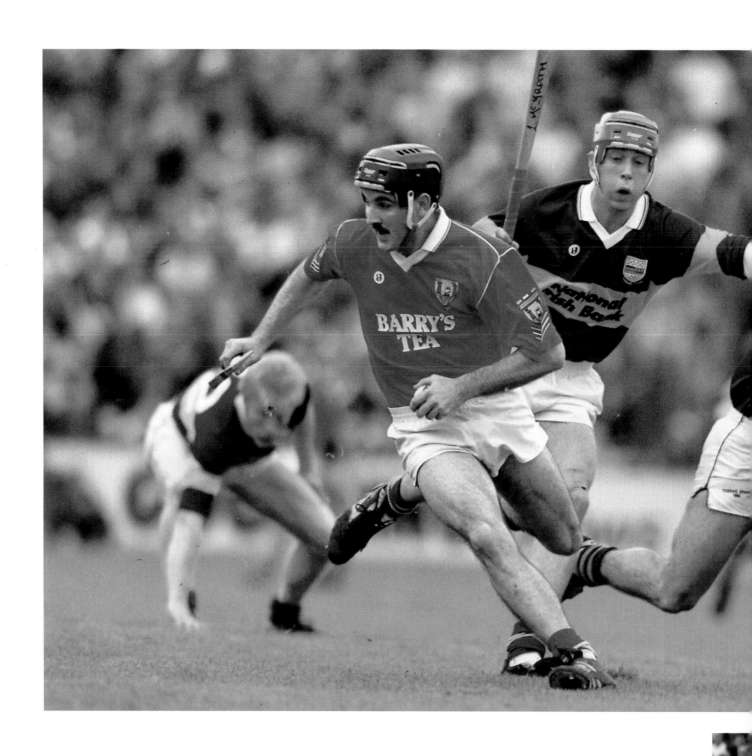

*C*ome gather round me boys tonight and raise your glasses high;
   Come Rockies, Barrs, and Rovers Stars, let welcome hit the sky;
   Let bonfire blaze in heroes' praise, let Shannon echoes fling
For homeward bound with hurling crown comes gallant Christy Ring.

How oft I've watched him from the hill move here and there in grace,
In Cork, Killarney, Thurles town or by the Shannon's race;
'Now Cork is bet; the hay is saved!' the thousands wildly sing-
They speak too soon, my sweet garsún, for here comes Christy Ring

(from "A Song for Christy Ring" by Bryan MacMahon)

*I*t is something like that of the Doge of Venice's wedding at Sea. A set of worthy Gentlemen, who have formed themselves into a body which they call the Water Club., proceed a few leagues out to sea once a year in a number of little vessels, which for painting and gilding exceed the King's yachts at Deptford and Greenwich. Their Admiral, who is elected annually, and hoists his flag on board his little vessel, leads the van, and receives the honours of the flag.

The rest of the fleet fall in their proper stations and keep their line in the same manner as the King's ships. This fle[et] is attended by a prodigious number of boats which, with their colours flying, drums beating, and trumpets sounding, forms one of the most agreeable and splendid sights your Lordship can conceive.

(The Royal Cork Yacht Club described in 1748 in "A Tour Through Ireland" and quoted in "Lovely is the Lee" by Robert Gibbings)

*A*t the high Window, shipping from all over the world
  Being borne up and down the busy, yet contemplative river;
  Skylines drifting in and out of skylines in the cloudy valley;
Firelight at dusk, and city lights in the high window,
Beyond them the control tower of the airport on the hill
- A lighthouse in the sky flashing green to white to green;
Our black and white cat snoozing in the corner of a chair;
(from "Windfalls, 8 Parnell Hill, Cork" from "The Berlin Wall Cafe"
by Paul Durcan, Belfast, 1985)

The new era did not dawn gently. Once again fire was the element which changed Cork and forged its modern facade. In 1920 the city endured a night of reprisal rioting and burning by British army irregulars (the notorious Black and Tans) which reduced much of the main business and commercial centre to rubble, especially Patrick Street, the central thoroughfare.

Rebuilt and reborn, Cork's expansion was accelerated at different times and in different ways during the next seventy years. An industrial park was established on a river-side site between the city and the suburb of Blackrock as early as 1917; now the chief industrial complexes lie outside the city environs, land-banks acquired during the last half-century allowing concentrations of specialised developments, with the proliferation of chemical industry in the lower harbour and many associated smaller plants being the most important ingredient in the modernisation of the greater Cork area.

Approaching the year 2,000 is no bad time for this city to re-assess its identity, its progress, its capacity for change and expansion. Today Cork unites in its administrative focus the energies of modern Europe with the traditions of its own past; it is a balancing act, but it is not only in reference to its medieval wall that it can be described as a gateway city.

The heritage of appreciation of the old is allied to an openness to the new; although Cork's expansion for generations seemed linked with particular enterprises - not all of which withstood the variations of war, politics or fashion - what has grown as a central economic identity is a thriving business, legal and commercial core, with industry filling up the gaps left by centralised bureaucracy and concentrated commerce. This has become a place in which the ordinary civic things are done with the intention of doing them not just well, but better.

As in the modern history of other countries and other towns, Cork suffered the acceleration of pernicious trends in terms of the loss of traditional jobs and the dislocation of traditional accommodation patterns and their replacement by purpose built housing estates which take several generations to become neighbourhoods. Yet if Cork could not escape the social dysfunction which is part of the modern European urban experience, the city has also benefited through its appreciation of Europe's strong urban consciousness.

Where there are problems there have to be solutions and increasingly those solutions are less imposed and more generated, informed by internal patterns of awareness, loyalties and aspiration rather than from external or national policy. Increasingly the power to shape one's own community is being understood.

The influence of the leading educational bodies, from University College to the Regional Technical College, from the College of Art and Design and the School of Music to the School of Commerce, has contributed enormously to the success of contemporary Cork.

The word infrastructure implies a solid base of administrative, transport and technical resources, and it is to providing such a core facility and indeed to making it synonymous with the city's growth that Cork's creative municipal energy has been devoted. Growth implies movement; the relationships between roads, services and community advancement are acknowledged in a lengthy linked series of new road systems allowing easier access both to the city's premier locations and to the countryside beyond. These also provide essential links to the national road system so that the air, rail and sea-borne traffic has an easy channel to the rest of Ireland.

The first underwater traffic- tunnel in Ireland will bring travellers quickly from one side of the harbour to the other, from the scenic routes to West Cork, Kerry and Limerick to the dense city-scapes and ports of the east coast and the fast routes northward.

evitalisation and enhancement have been the prime civic strategies, implying aggressive proposals for job creation and a dedicated search, and research, for employment opportunities and long-term manufacturing commitments. The major local educational establishments have devised programmes which, time after time, echo the municipal preoccupations of the city and of the country.

It is no great surprise, for example, that the food sciences are significant study areas at University College, Cork, where both the Faculty of Food Science and Technology and the National Food Biotechnology Centre operate as international centres for education, research and training for an industry which harnesses traditional resources with the most contemporary developments in both production and marketing.

Equally, business studies and the departments of commerce and computer sciences maintain relationships which have distinguished Cork through the years. Even more indicative, though, of the college's educational commitment to the expanding opportunities of the international scientific and industrial environment is the National Microelectronic Research Centre - located, in another example of inspired preservation, in the old river-side maltings buildings of an otherwise vanished brewery. This, like the National Power Electronics Research Laboratory and the Telecommunications Microwave Laboratory (designated as the national centre of expertise in high-frequency and micro-wave electronics) ensures that UCC's budget is continually enhanced by major national and international research contracts.

Educationally innovative and linked to all the city's important activities, from the teaching hospitals to the concerts and theatres ,from sports to adult education and social administration, UCC is part of an infrastructure which includes the dynamism of the Regional Technical College, another institution crucial to industrial and commercial recruitment in the city. This relationship is particularly enriching to Cork, since it allows inter-disciplinary and inter-faculty movement and also provides opportunities of artistic cross-fertilisation through the fusion between the RTC's constituent colleges such as the School of Music and the College of Art and Design.

Such linkages help to maintain the cultural ethos as well as the educational one and contribute to the prominence of the Cork Symphony Orchestra, the Vanburgh String Quartet, the Crawford Gallery of Art, the City Museum, the Cork Archive Institute, the National Sculpture Factory, the theatres, concert halls and art centres and galleries.

Another massive ingredient in the expansion of Cork has been the role of the Harbour Commissioners, forming, with Cork Corporation and Cork County Council, the administrative triumvirate which has managed the complex modern organism which is the harbour through the last seventy years. The harbour itself is a resource, as driven, designed and aggressive as any municipal unit can be while remaining something of a natural force. The port of Cork has always been a huge economic factor in the history of the city; now, as well as providing the safe harbour for ships which has remained its central dedication, the port is an industrial focus for the city and the harbour towns have developed to meet the demands of this relocation.

Nothing happens by accident. There is opportunity, there is the native entrepreneur, and there is planning. A solid commercial basis in the city, where the financial infrastructure is now less local and more international than the merchant bankers of the South Mall could ever have envisaged as they ticked off the bills of lading from the ships returning from a Carribbean voyage, has underpinned the relationships between central financial disposition and local enterprise.

The physical growth of the city is managed by City Hall with an eye to the need to keep the core vibrant yet free- flowing, to the imperatives of preservation and restoration, and to its own relationships with private developers and the housing and commercial needs of the greater community.

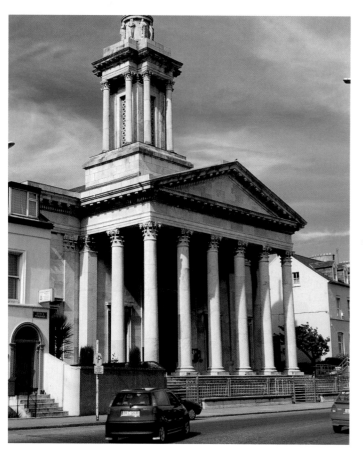

The economic challenge of attracting the big players in a highly competitive environment is part of the strategy which ensures the survival of the city's prosperous personality, and one which marches with national agencies charged with that responsibility on a wider basis.

The success of these efforts is indicated in the number of national organisations which have chosen Cork as their headquarters, such as An Bord Gais, the national gas board, or the Central Statistics Office, or tenants of the various industrial or business and technology parks, or any of the more than fifty companies in the electronics and information technology industry, or those corporations which have accepted the city as their premier business location.

There are two great breweries now attached to international titles such as Fosters and Heineken; there is Irish Distillers at Midleton and renowned names in the international pharmaceutical industry, property developers whose remit has an all-Ireland scope.

At the same time every chance of enhancing the potential of smaller, indigenous or traditional industries and businesses has to be grasped. Business enhancement schemes have been carefully applied and incentives allocated where opportunities for revitalisation can be created. Dairy and agricultural enterprises flourish on the outskirts of the city while remaining part of its economic identity - and of its future.

The outskirts: if Cork is a gateway, what lies beyond its landlocked boundaries? What traces remain now of the Kings of Fermoy, or the Chieftains of Carbery? And where, once the traveller's eyes reach the summits of the hills which ring the city, should the journey reach?

*O*ur illustrious visitor availed himself of the leisure moments in the intervals of his entertainments to visit the scenery in the vicinity of Cork, having gone yesterday to Queenstown, and this day to Blarney. He spent a quarter of an hour on the top of the Castle, surveying the pleasant prospect, and before departing kissed the famous stone. Whether Mr. Dickens thought this ceremonial necessary to increase the magic with which his tongue is tipped we do not know...

(Charles Dickens in Cork, from The Cork Examiner, September 1st, 1858)

*O*ne of Cork County's most famous buildings, the castle at Blarney is still spoken of as a stronghold of the McCarthy line which ruled what was then the Kingdom of South Munster.

KINSALE

The kind of rain we knew is a thing of the past --
deep-delving, dark, deliberate you would say,
browsing on spire and bogland; but today
our sky-blue slates are steaming in the sun,
our yachts tinkling and dancing in the bay
like race-horses. We contemplate at last
shining windows, a future forbidden to no-one.

(Derek Mahon, Selected Poetry, London 1995)

*T*hrough the slush of the limestone tracks and the
 sopping field-paths they are cantering past the viaduct
 into town... A deadly day, with a kind of tunnel-vapour, over the puddles
of St. Mary's of the Isle, and the swamps of the Grand Parade giving off fogs
and gas. And so the foremost rider swears and shouts and wonders who dug
this town out, and whether the natives of it are web-footed from so much
floundering in the wet. For he is a man never beaten anywhere by wind or
enemy... Until the rain! rain! rain! and January 1649, and his fleet at Kinsale
for the Stuarts again. Wherefore now this new Alexander, Prince Rupert his
name, pestered with another fleet blockading him inside the old Head, rides in at
the gate of Cork to beg food for his men most awkwardly cut off.

(The South Gate from "The Glamour of Cork", by D.L. Kelleher, 1919)

The next question at issue is, does Cork City owe its existence to the Danish and the Norse settlements in the flat of the river ?. A glance at any modern atlas of Europe, noting especially all the river mouths and harbours would convince even the most sceptical that it would be a peculiar exception if no town existed somewhere within the precincts of Cork Harbour..... The particular place Cork Harbour holds in order of merit among all European Harbours is not a question of prime importance, but superlative terms may be applied to the degree of excellence it possesses, without fear of contradiction.

(from "The Economic History of Cork" Wm. O'Sullivan, 1937)

Steady, now! for our distant goal,
*   Put forth your strength as our boat returns;*
*   Like the dawn of Faith o'er the trusting soul,*
The beacon-light in the Castle burns.
Remember bright eyes gaze on you,
And watch our boat with throbbing breast;
Then cheerily, cheerily, gallant crew!
When the prize is won we'll sweetly rest.
Row together bold and free,
Though the pulses glow and the sinews strain;
For the ever-sparkling River Lee,
The name we have won we'll still retain.

(from "The Lee Club Regatta Song"
by John Fitzgerald 1913)

1297 *(June 15th) To the receiver for the victualling of the King of England in Gascony William de Moans Chamberlain of the Exchequer in Dublin Etc. Greeting we send to you for the support of the army in Gascony from the Vil of Cork in the ship which is called "the Snake" whose master is Simon le White, 140 quarters of corn, London measure........*

(from Caulfield's Council Book of Cork)

eeking no solitude, fearing no danger,
Swiftly and gracefully onward they glide-
Out in the sunshine, unheeding the stranger,
Sail the white birds on the Lee's flashing tide.
Not in deep pools underneath the sad willow,
Where the children of Lir rested far from the sea;
But fighting with gulls for the waifs of the billow,
Undaunted and proud, go the swans of the Lee.

(from "The Swans of the Lee" by John Fitzgerald)

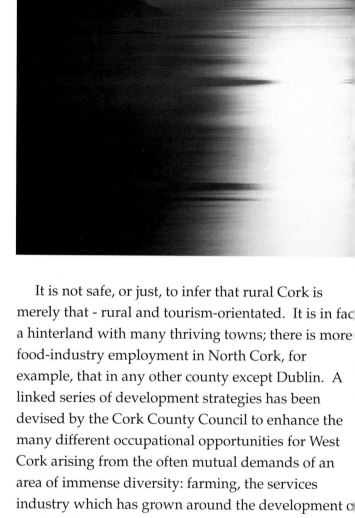

*A*nd sure it is yet a most beautiful and sweet country as any is under heaven, being stored throughout with many goodly rivers, replenished with all sorts of fish most abundantly, sprinkled with many sweet islands, and goodly lakes, like little inland seas, which will carry even ships on their waters, adorned with goodly woods, even fit for the building of houses and ships so commodiously, as that if some princes of the world had them they would soon hope to be lords of all the seas, and ere long of all the world; and also full of very good ports and havens... besides the soil itself most fertile, fit to yield all kinds of fruits, that shall be committed thereunto.

And lastly, the heavens most mild and temperate, though somewhat more moist in the parts towards the west."

Although it must sometimes seem that what Edmund Spenser called the parts towards the west dominate images of the Cork landscape there is not a townland in the county which does not invite the attention of the traveller. It is a large county, the largest in Ireland; the scenic attractions are various, sometimes dramatic.

Everywhere local communities have identified aspects of their own ethos or tradition and built restorative programmes which also invite the visitor to linger even in small townlands where nothing much seems to move apart from a winding stream.

It is not safe, or just, to infer that rural Cork is merely that - rural and tourism-orientated. It is in fact a hinterland with many thriving towns; there is more food-industry employment in North Cork, for example, that in any other county except Dublin. A linked series of development strategies has been devised by the Cork County Council to enhance the many different occupational opportunities for West Cork arising from the often mutual demands of an area of immense diversity: farming, the services industry which has grown around the development of tourism, the needs of the fishing community, the islands and the coastal villages, the small arts and craft groupings - and with all these must be considered the needs of such towns as Bantry or Clonakilty, Skibbereen or Dunmanway or Castletownbere.

To the north and east there is the dramatic valley of the Blackwater, a river which spans the county and enters the sea at Youghal; its bordering lands are pastoral and then mountainous, its burden one of history interwoven with the daily life of centuries of farming. It flows through the towns of Mallow and Fermoy until, sliding into County Waterford through the Comeragh Mountains and making its dramatic turn at Cappoquin, it re-enters Cork to reach the sea at Youghal. The great mountains here are the Galtees and Knockmealdowns; they lie towards the eastern edge, lifting in heathered ridges above Mitchelstown and shadowing the main road to Dublin. North and west the Boggeragh Mountains hide Millstreet and Kanturk and the beginnings of that vast plain from which the Province of Munster drew its agricultural wealth, The Golden Vale.

Marking the edges of this valley lie the small ranges of the Ballyhouras, the Nagles and the Kilworth Mountains. This is the landscape which inspired the novels of Canon Sheehan and which was immortalised by Elizabeth Bowen in "Bowen's Court". It is the landscape which harboured Spenser at Kilcolman. Linked by tributaries, its pleasures range from Kilworth to Newmarket, from Charleville and Doneraile and Castletownroche to the gardens at Anne's Grove and the sheltered meadows of Castlelyons and Ballynoe.

These lie south-east of Fermoy and trace the routes back through Ballyvolane and Dungourney to Midleton. There is good river fishing here and a growing business in sea angling. The terrain is gentle, the fields profitable, the villages hospitable and full of character.

Their charm is serenity, yet these places and their people are not passive. There has been a long engagement with the land and with the sea. The small harbour of Ballycotton is famous for its fish and its sea angling and lies close to Cloyne where philosopher Bishop George Berkeley lived and worked from 1734 to 1753. A few miles away is Shanagarry where the Penn family were given a grant of land by Charles ll; here lived for a time the young William Penn who became a Quaker during a visit to Cork and who went on to give his name to Pennsylvania.

If there are good country house restaurants and hotels throughout Ireland - and there are - It is largely due to Myrtle and Ivan Allen of Ballymaloe House, an internationally renowned hotel which developed from Myrtle's desire to make the best use of the produce of the family farm and of the fishermen at Ballycotton. From this in turn came the cookery school at Shanagarry founded by Darina and Tim Allen, which sends its graduates every year to spread a culinary gospel of freshness, quality and superb cuisine.

Throughout County Cork there are enterprises such as these. Another is at Millstreet where a town has turned a fondness for horses into an international equestrian landmark which is also a venue for major sporting and entertainment events, from Eurovision to world boxing championships. Everywhere - Ballyhoura is another example - the people have turned their attention to enhancing the properties of each region, although there can be few examples to rival Kinsale, the small ancient port to the south of Cork city which has re-fashioned itself as a place of great architectural interest and as a gourmet mecca. Another town close to Cork both physically and emotionally is Cobh, the former Queenstown, a transatlantic port with a position on the edge of Cork harbour which has ensured its place in history through the ages. And there is Youghal, thirty miles to the east on the borders of County Waterford, the mouth of the Blackwater and a thriving town of beaches and promenades and funfairs on one side and on the other presenting an almost untouched facade of Georgian and Victorian street-scapes, its two most prominent features being the clock tower of 1777 and the lighthouse set between the main road and the sea.

The county of Cork abounds with recreational inducements. Traditional sports such as hunting, fishing, shooting, road-bowling and sailing are on offer for participation or for spectacle. Golf, greyhound racing and sports centres lengthen a list which includes, in the city itself, pigeon-racing. There is horse-racing at Mallow and Limerick Junction, and it is easier than ever before to walk and swim and climb for those who love to match their activity to the lie of the land.

Near the city are the villages which have grown about the harbour. There are the yacht clubs and the beaches and all the amenities a large urban

population creates for the enjoyment of its leisure. And it is not for nothing that Cork has won itself the title of Festival City, with weekends devoted to international celebrations of choral music or jazz, or a week-long festival of film, another of youth theatre, a festival of folk music, garden visits, summer colleges. Conferences and seminars of scientific, commercial, legal, medical and educational concerns occur regularly in the city's annual calendar, and as with any city, Cork has a cultural wealth to be enjoyed.

Yet it is still to the west of the county that the magic-seeking eye returns, to the bordering highlands that separate Cork and Kerry and which give birth to the county's two major rivers, the Lee and the Blackwater. The wealth of folklore and literature, tradition and happening, which clings to every acre of this landscape is probably no uncommon inheritance, yet to leave Bandon on one road or Macroom on the other route westwards is to enter a pathway forever beckoning, forever hinting at the hills beyond the beyond. Bantry Bay, Dunmanus, Roaringwater, the headlands and peninsulas, Carbery's hundred isles, the Miskish, Caha and Derrynasaggart mountains, the rocky inlets of Adrigole and Allihies, Ahakista and Kilcrohane, the beaches of Barley Cove and Crookhaven, the little reed-edged lakes at Inchigeelagh - all make up a litany of enchantment which has not tarnished with the new traffic.

There are other pleasures here: concerts at Bantry House or at the church of St.Barrahane in Castletownshend, made famous by its organist Edith Oenone Somerville and her cousin Violet Martin (Ross); there are arts and crafts exhibitions at the West Cork Arts Centre in Skibbereen, a model village in Clonakilty which is in itself something of a model town. Good restaurants, some famous, occur throughout the region, especially at Ballylickey near Glengarriff, at Baltimore and Schull and Durrus and at Dunworley near Clonakilty. There are great gardens - Timoleague and Creagh the most remarkable among them - and excellent, character-full hotels, hostels and guest-houses.

The place-names resound. Pretty pictures, most of them. But Cork also has a cultural hinterland, and these names are not mere scenic playgrounds.

Modern literature and scholarship enshrine ancient memory, and it is possible now to understand something of what that hinterland once held in terms of its society, its living ethos, its bardic schools, its courts of poetry, its legends and its music-makers.

The old Ireland, the countryside of the Irish language, was in touch with the richest sources of European influence. Munster was a province profoundly affected by an intellectual traffic of such intensity that even its hedge schools used Greek and Latin. To rove the western borders of the county of Cork, to stroll through the groves of Blarney, to wander among the hills beyond Youghal or ponder the headstones in the ruined abbey of Timoleague is to set foot in what Daniel Corkery described as the hidden Ireland.

Sometimes a gateway has a mystical function. Sometimes an entrance can be effected in an almost spiritual way, as if a door were more than locks and handles, a window more than glass and casement. For the traveller, the visitor, the native with some depth of vision, Cork offers another revelation: a route to a particular heritage, a landscape as mysterious, as dense and as beautiful as anything visible or palpable. A modern city, Cork is a gateway to the past as well as to the future.

We gratefully acknowledge the help of many people in the preparation of this book, and especially the following:

Greg Delanty for permission to use "Setting the Type" from *"Southward"* (Dublin 1992)
The estate of Eilís Dillon for extracts from her translation of "Caoineadh Airt Ui Laoghaire"
Theo Dorgan for "Long Valley Vignette" from the *"Ordinary House of Love"* (Galway 1990)
Paul Durcan for an extract from "Windfall, 8 Parnell Hill, Cork" from *"The Berlin Wall Cafe"*, (Belfast 1985)
Cork University Press and Patrick Galvin for extracts from "The Madwoman of Cork" from *"The Woodburners"* (1973)
Laurence Pollinger Ltd. and the estate of Robert Gibbings for extracts from *"Lovely is the Lee"* (London 1944) and *"Sweet Cork of Thee"* (London 1952)
Isabel Healy for extracts from "A Cork Girlhood from *"The Cork Anthology "*(Cork 1993)
Marianne Heron for extracts from *"The Hidden Gardens of Ireland"* (Dublin 1996)
Bryan McMahon for an extract from "The Ballad of Christy Ring"
Gallery Press and Derek Mahon for "Kinsale" from *"Antarctica"* (Loughcrew 1985)
Thomas McCarthy for an extract from *"The Non-Aligned Storyteller"* (London, 1984)
Harriet Sheehy and the estate of Frank O'Connor for extracts from *"An Only Child"* (London 1961);
Rogers Coleridge and White Ltd. and the estate of Seán Ó Faoláin for extracts from *"Vive Moi"* (London 1965)
Caoimhín Ó Marcaig and the estate of Seán Ó Ríordain for "Cúl an Tí" from *"Eireaball Spideoige"* (1952)
Cork University Press for extracts from "The Economic History of Cork from Earliest Times to the Act of Union" by William O'Sullivan (Cork 1937)
Seán Ó Tuama for extracts from "Caoineadh Airt Ui Laoghaire" from "An Duanaire" (Mountrath 1981)

Our thanks also for their help and co-operation to the staff of Boole Library, University College Cork, Cork City Library, Cork County Library, the Photographic Library at Examiner Publications and the Manuscript Department of the British Library.